Practice of the Presence of God with Devotional & Study Guide

Brother Lawrence

21st Century Version, Guide & Commentaries
by J. D. Nelson

Permissions

Efforts have been made to indicate required permissions or be within fair use guidelines for quotations. This adaptation, interpretation and translation of material arises from works in the public domain. If any appropriate acknowledgements have been omitted or rights overlooked, please notify writer and publisher so subsequent editions may be corrected.

Johansson Garcia Publishing
World Literature Division

I have recreated events from my memories. Names, businesses, places, chronologies and identifying details have been changed to protect the privacy of individuals who are often composites of people. Any resemblance to actual persons, living or dead, or actual events is purely coincidental.

Contents

Foreword

Living With God

I first met Brother Lawrence and the *Practice of the Presence of God* when I was 19 and in college. I had moved from what some might consider a backward and countrified town in the west to a big city in the northeast for college. The school was not a friendly place. Courses were difficult. I did not find a community within which to fit. I was having difficulty adjusting to that new place and environment. Lawrence's simple and profound message was an epiphany. God the Father, Jesus and the Holy Spirit became my tangible and present three person community.

"If we would enjoy the peace of paradise even within this life, we must accustom ourselves to a familiar, humble and affectionate conversation with Him. We must stop our spirit from wandering away from Him upon any occasion. We must make our heart a spiritual temple where we adore Him incessantly." [14th Letter, below.] I tried to follow Lawrence's teaching and guidance in practicing the presence of God in my daily life. I tried to do so as I went to classes, studied and interacted with friends and acquaintances.

Despite the challenges I faced in college, it was a time in my life when I was filled with curiosity, wonder and excitement about the great, wide world, about all that was happening and new in my life. I was amazed at the complexity and intriguing nature of God's Creation and magnificent universe. I sensed God's presence within the world, in all that I saw and read. It was extraordinary. I browsed in the reserve room of the library which had copies of classic texts for many disciplines: literature, history, anthropology, biology and American studies. I wandered among the shelves and pulled out and read parts of seminal works while standing in the middle of an aisle or sitting at a nearby window, glancing out upon the day.

I would browse and read on Friday and Saturday afternoons in the library for a few hours when there was no press of work that was due the next day. I lay on campus lawns and read short stories and poetry. Sun played upon the flickering leaves of the trees. I spoke with and projected my thoughts to God about all that I saw and read. I was amazed at all that was sublime, at the diversity of the world and my ability to touch pieces of humanity within those who were from startlingly different periods of time and backgrounds. I was able to glimpse grace in what others had experienced and written. I found beautiful places from which to celebrate.

I walked and jogged with God through my college and the adjoining neighborhoods, along a river and through a large city park. I felt His breath and touch upon me and experienced ineffable joy. Not just in the magnificent natural world of trees and meadows with their singing songbirds and mischievous squirrels, but among desolate neighborhoods of a brown and gray city, and silent and frowning storefronts and human beings. O Lord, your face is beautiful and grave to me…

I sensed His glory and presence everywhere I roamed, in all that I saw; and gained fear and awe for His person. I felt a pure awareness and excitement about living in the presence of God the Father, the Holy Spirit and Jesus Christ. I prayed and celebrated and danced like David, with God, wherever I was, within whatever I was doing.

Those were my first moments of unity with God and inter-living with His three persons. Any common day could be made joyful and exalted in His presence. Practicing the presence of God repaired and reformed my relationship with God, and renewed my soul. It made me understand the revolutionary nature of unity with the persons of God, and the revolutionary discipleship which was required of my life. Ultimately, God made my being stronger and more tranquil, and helped me establish myself within certain groups and activities at my college. I made friends and learned lessons which would last a lifetime.

Job Loss and Hardship

The recent Great Recession affected many within my local community and church, as well as many of my friends and acquaintances across the country. I saw and heard about profound hardship and pain--from the loss of jobs and loss of a home to illness, medical bills and family instability. Fathers, mothers and children experienced extraordinary suffering. There was depression and anxiety; the abuse of alcohol and drugs. There was homelessness and hunger; divorce and separation from children. The swath of destruction was breathtaking.

I was reminded by some of these events of my experience of being laid off from a job a number of years ago (before the Great Recession and before my marriage and children). I still remember clearly when and how I was told, and the days and weeks which followed. I felt great fatigue and malaise initially, which seemed to evolve into dejection and sadness. I had difficulty understanding and internalizing what happened, getting my head around the very simple fact that I had been laid off. I would keep coming back at it, consider it from different angles, with puzzlement. It was difficult to leave behind.

In that more distant era, my colleagues and I who lost our jobs did not speak about what occurred, did not share or find mutual understanding or support. It seemed a matter for embarrassment and shame. We had never thought of ourselves as people who might be laid off or fired. I notice there has been much greater mutual support and networking among those affected by the Great Recession, explicit discussion of what happened and why, the sharing of stories, compassion and kinship and help.

I applied for jobs, networked and had a couple interviews over a long period of time. I applied for many jobs I knew I could never get; just to feel like I was doing something constructive. I would think I fit a job description, or had a good meeting, and then I would hear nothing. The company and its various personnel would not reply when I reached out to them. Let me know something, one way or another, I would pray.

I would be awakened in the early mornings by my anxiety, by my thoughts and worries. I would try to empty my mind, to think of nothing, so I could somehow get back to sleep again. I lay in bed, arched my body, stretched out my arms and cried to God. And He would be there, holding me. I have had friends, then and since, who have been without work for years at a time, searching for a job without success. There is an extraordinary desolation which arises.

During that period, I enjoyed being with close friends, not necessarily talking about my job loss and its consequences, but simply being with those who knew me well, who listened and spoke with understanding and empathy. Over time, many of my friends gained spouses and children, significant job responsibilities. We all became more separate and removed from each other than we had been when we were single. All of us developed our own complex lives and were less available for each other than we had been previously. I spoke with my parents and obtained comfort from their support and prayers.

But in the end, God and His three persons were my most constant company and solace. They understood my hardships and heartaches, and all my complicated feelings, anxieties and hopes like no other. I would converse with all three of them, and there would be simple joys and laughter as I shared my thoughts and hopes, my life, with them, as I grilled meat and vegetables for dinner, or went to the beach or a park and watched and listened to people living their lives.

Brother Lawrence encourages us to thank God for suffering, illness, burdens which God may allow in our lives. It has frequently been difficult for me to genuinely thank God for bad things which have happened in my life. I doubt if I have done so in any way that has impressed Him. It has not, however, been difficult to see how hardship has led me forward within God's will, and toward maturity and submission. It has been an extreme consolation, a matter of survival, to have God the Father, the Holy Spirit and Jesus surround and embrace me consistently and constantly during all those difficult times.

In my situation with my loss of a job, there was no easy solution, no dream employment which fell into my lap. However, I was fortunate to have the ability to return home to live with my parents, go on to graduate school and start a new life and occupation.

Inconsistency, Sin and Distraction

Even after experiencing God's presence regularly, after experiencing extraordinary joy, satisfaction and fulfillment, I have fallen away from God. Because of sin, distraction, laziness, bad habits. How can I be such a fool? It surprises and amazes me that God is as forgiving and compassionate as He is, and so constant. When I return to Him with sin, disobedience, inconsistency; when I return mangy, unkempt and smelling of refuse, I have been embraced, restored and reclaimed. I am amazed by His love, His mercy, His shocking humility. I return with baggage and burdens, and God is willing to relieve me of them. I am ashamed and slow to look Him in the face, but speak with Him, confess my sins and thank Him for his grace. I have faith that God will always have His hand upon me, and that He will never give up on me.

After my marriage and the arrival of children, the days have frequently become hectic and stressful. My wife works and the children are in school and have extracurricular activities. It can be difficult to feel like one is in the presence of God with all the various individuals in the family running in different directions. It has been only on rare occasions that it has seemed like all of us have been aware at the same time of God's presence: On a pleasant Sunday when we are all in a row singing *How Great Thou Art*. During the season of the birth of our Lord Jesus Christ, when presents are forgotten, and we are sitting in our warm family room about a fresh and piney Douglas fir twinkling with lights, talking and laughing. When we are at the ocean feeling the warm sun and breeze upon our bodies, or experience the mighty power of the waves tossing us all like flotsam back and about. They are beautiful moments indeed.

I am trying, and our family must try with God's help to become more consistent and aware of Him in our common and daily lives. In the devotional and study guide I provide an example of a schedule which may assist an individual, as well as an individual and a family, cultivate the practice of the presence of God on a daily basis.

Introduction

Origins

Brother Lawrence was born Nicholas Herrman in the region of Lorraine in eastern France into a family of peasants. The date of his birth has been listed variously as 1611 and 1614, and his death as in 1691. Nicholas was quite poor growing up, and he joined the army in order to obtain regular meals and earn a small income.

He fought in the Thirty Years War which was a particularly destructive series of wars occurring in central Europe between 1618 and 1648. The fighting was often between armies of mercenaries and resulted in extraordinary violence and millions of casualties, both military and civilian. It began as a conflict between Protestant and Catholic states, and evolved to be less about religion and more into a struggle over which states would be the superpowers of the era.

Nicholas was wounded in the fighting, with certain sources indicating injuries to a leg and subsequent difficulties with walking and chronic pain. He left the army and served as a servant to a person of eminence.

Religious Order

Nicholas later joined the Discalced Carmelite Priory in Paris as a lay brother, and took the name of Lawrence of the Resurrection. Discalced means without shoes, and this Catholic religious order was established in 1593 and adopted a lifestyle of poverty and emphasized prayer and contemplation. It was created as part of a reform movement initiated by Teresa of Avila and John of the Cross in Spain. Both were sublime thinkers and writers who believed in cultivating a profound personal intimacy with Jesus Christ.

Within the priory, Nicholas worked in the kitchen initially and later as a repairer of sandals. His character and demeanor, his way of life and holiness caught the attention of many, including members of the church hierarchy. A notable cleric, the Abbe Joseph de Beaufort, who became vicar general to the Archbishop of Paris, interviewed Brother Lawrence over several conversations. De Beaufort compiled the content of what was to become *Practice the Presence of God* after the death of Brother Lawrence. The book is composed of notes of the conversations de Beaufort had with Brother Lawrence as well as letters Brother Lawrence wrote to various individuals on the same subject.

Spiritual Journey and Practice of the Presence of God

At about the age of 18 Nicholas had a dramatic spiritual experience which he described as acquainting him with God's sovereignty and nature. What is interesting is that his profound experience was founded within a very simple and everyday matter. He saw a tree stripped of its leaves in the winter, and thought that within a short time the leaves would be renewed, and after that flowers and fruit appear. In that simple realization, he sensed the grandeur and sovereignty of God over all the world. He indicated that sense and conviction was never gone from his soul subsequently. He stated that realization set him loose from the concerns and ties of the world, and kindled in him a wonderful and great love for God, and a desire to serve Him. That profound meaning of commonplace occurrences which are nevertheless quite significant for Brother Lawrence continues throughout the book. Lawrence speaks of doing something as mundane, necessary and common as picking up a piece of straw from the ground, and doing it in God's presence, for and unto Him.

Martin Luther, in his exposition of Psalm 147, emphasized the significance of work as a vocation and calling which included daily secular and mundane activities. He indicated God worked through His children, through their jobs, roles, activities. The individual honors God and loves his neighbor by serving and loving through his work. As illustrated above, Brother Lawrence often sees and analyzes on an even more microscopic level. Every second and every little thing he does and thinks about can be for and with God, in His Presence. This served to establish a life of peace, meaning, sacredness and transcendence within Lawrence.

In his writing, Brother Lawrence reflects humility, and occasionally, a gentle, self deprecating humor. He recognized that obtaining the practice of the presence of God was not easy. It took him time and effort, and importantly, habituation, over the course of years. There is repetition in what is presented within the book, within the conversations and letters, but there tends to be different nuances emphasized and new substance added. Brother Lawrence is a child of God with a distinct experience, personality and character. He makes certain comments which reflect his human and imperfect nature as all of us do, even as much of what he discusses or writes has universal truths and applications. The material and concepts of Brother Lawrence's work and book have had a profound effect over the centuries on innumerable men and women.

Approach

I wanted to make *Practice of the Presence of God* easier to read and understand, and accessible to a wider readership for the 21st Century. I also wanted to actively engage with the text and weave it into my being in a different way from the passive reading I had done for many years. Creating this version has allowed me to do that. I have tried to retain a certain poetry and rhythm of the original works, and there are times when I sacrifice grammar and other rules to approach the voice and cadence of the original material. Nevertheless, I have tried to make the text clear and easily understandable in modern day language.

30 Day Devotional & Study Guide

Techniques and Strategies

I have found it beneficial to go over this book and material periodically in my life. It has been useful to do so in small segments and as a devotional. That method has helped make it a habit, integrating concepts and principles over an extended period of time. I have provided a 30 day devotional guide and plan below which is consistent with this idea.

It has also been helpful to go through this material with a partner or small group. More and greater insights can be gleaned with discussion. It can be critical to have mutual commitment, energy and accountability for implementing the principles of the practice of the presence of God. I have provided questions for reflection and discussion in the guide below.

Daily Schedule Example to Cultivate God's Presence:

Daily personal devotions
Family/Individual morning prayers
Mid-morning prayer and meditation
Lunchtime prayer and meditation
Mid-afternoon prayer and meditation
Dinner with family/self in God's presence
Family/Individual devotions and prayers

The above schedule can be used to consciously and habitually cultivate and return to God's presence and converse with Him throughout a busy day, in all one's work and activities. Start with time you can responsibly devote, and you will often find you have more time than you realize. You will find yourself conversing with Him constantly and continually. I find myself becoming more peaceful and productive within my spiritual life as well as my working and family lives when I am able to become habitual in conversing with God in a consistent and disciplined manner. Even two or a few minutes for each of the entries above can have a remarkable effect.

Use all the five basic senses, of sight, hearing, touch, smell and taste, to cultivate greater awareness of God's presence, within His magnificent Creation, in everyday life and among all places and matters. Speak with and convey your thoughts and feelings to God constantly.

Actively welcome and converse with God. Meet Him and all that is about you consciously with warmth and love and empathy. Use regular breathing and relaxation to meditate and pray. Be mindful of your body and what it senses, and of your mind and what it feels and thinks. God will fill you with His Spirit.

Day1: Foreword and Introduction

1. Having read the Foreword and Introduction, what are goals you can pursue in reading the book?

Day 2: First Half of First Conversation

1. What are ways God's grandeur and sovereignty may have set Brother Lawrence loose from the ties of the world and created a great love for God?

2. What are ways to establish habits of conversing constantly or frequently with God?

Day 3: Second Half of First Conversation

1. What are important aspects of faith?
2. How can you resign yourself to God's will?

Day 4: First Third of Second Conversation

1. How can one make the love of God one's constant motive?
2. How can you overcome fear and anxiety and live in freedom and joy?

Day 5: Middle Third of Second Conversation

1. How can you make a habit of confessing to God in your day?
2. What are ways you can live simply with God in your daily life?

Day 6: Last Third of Second Conversation

1. What are specific ways in which you can trust in God, and take all your cares to Him?
2. How can you cultivate the practice of praying constantly?

Day 7: First Half of Third Conversation

1. How can you develop fear and awe of God?
2. What are unusual activities during which you could practice God's presence?

Day 8: Second Half of Third Conversation

1. What are benefits of resignation to God's will?
2. Why does Brother Lawrence say there is little virtue in people?

Day 9: First Third of Fourth Conversation

1. How can you converse with God with freedom and simplicity?
2. How can you praise, adore and love God constantly?

Day 10: Middle Third of Fourth Conversation

1. How can you pursue holiness and sanctification daily?
2. How can you practice faith, hope and charity in your life?

Day 11: Last Third of Fourth Conversation

1. How can you pursue God's presence in your job?
2. What was the effect of Brother Lawrence's practices on his disposition and countenance?

Day 12: First Letter

1. What are methods by which Brother Lawrence cultivates God's presence?
2. What are results of cultivating God's presence?

Day 13: First Third of Second Letter

1. What are differences in the perspectives Brother Lawrence describes?
2. What are aspects of the faith described, both by Brother Lawrence and the notation?

Day 14: Second Third of Second Letter

1. What were some of the reasons for Brother Lawrence's difficulty for 10 years?
2. What are characteristics of his state of being?

Day 15: Last Third of Second Letter

1. How does God treat this 'most wretched' of men?
2. How does Lawrence see himself in God's presence?

Day 16: Third Letter

1. How can you find reassurance and fortitude during times of danger?

Day 17: First Half of Fourth Letter

1. How can you open your heart to God?
2. How can you find repose and rest, contentment and satisfaction?

Day 18: Second Half of Fourth Letter

1. What are barriers we put up to God?
2. Are you delaying renewal and fervor?

Day 19: Fifth Letter

1. Who do you pray for and how do you pray for them?
2. Have you had continual conversations with God for extended periods of time?

Day 20: Sixth Letter

1. Is it possible to take pleasures which are innocent and lawful and also with and in God?

2. How can you obtain greater freedom even as you serve God faithfully?

Day 21: Seventh Letter

1. How have the years affected your experience of your time with God?
2. Are you approaching God with confidence and humility?

Day 22: Eight Letter

1. What are patterns and weakness you have noticed in your own thinking and times of devotion?
2. Are you confessing and addressing your shortcomings in thinking?

Day 23: Ninth Letter

1. How does this letter say we can obtain God's help?
2. How can you think more about God?

Day 24: Tenth Letter

1. What has been your experience with loss of family or friends?
2. What has brought you closer to God in that context?

Day 25: Eleventh Letter

1. What has your experience been with God when you have been ill and in pain?
2. There are truths to what Lawrence says in this letter--how difficult is it to listen and integrate some of his comments?

Day 26: Twelfth Letter

1. What are different ways in which you can entertain yourself and God?
2. How is it that faith is our support and foundation?
3. Could there be scientific and spiritual truth in Lawrence's assertion that disease may be alleviated by practice of the presence of God?

Day 27: Thirteenth Letter

1. Is it wise to obtain counsel for health matters from physicians and clergy, family and friends?
2. How can one trust in God for solace and help in illness and pain?

Day 28: Fourteenth Letter

1. How can you obtain the peace of paradise on earth?
2. How can you persevere to obtain the right mindset?

Day 29: Fifteenth Letter

1. How should we view our burdens and suffering?
2. How can we seek and love God by faith, and not for reward?

Day 30: Please read the Afterword; and then identify two favorite truths or lessons learned from book.

First Conversation

(Between Brother Lawrence and the Abbe de Beaufort)

1. Conversion of Brother Lawrence
2. Prior Employment
3. Establish Ourselves in God's Presence Through Conversation

4. Faith is Our Duty
5. Resign Self to God's Will

The first time I saw Brother Lawrence was upon the 3rd of August, 1666.

He told me that God had done him the singular favor of causing his salvation at the age of eighteen.
This happened in the winter. He saw a tree stripped of its leaves, and realized that within a short time, the leaves would be renewed, and after that the flowers and fruit appear. He sensed the grandeur and sovereignty of God over all the world in that epiphany, and that understanding has never been gone from his soul since then. This set him loose from the ties of the world, and kindled in him such a great love for God, that he could not say whether it increased in the greater than forty years he lived subsequently.

Brother Lawrence had been footman to M. Fieubert, the [king's] treasurer, and described himself humorously as a great awkward fellow who broke everything.

He said he wished to be received into a monastery, thinking he would be made penitent for his awkwardness and the sins he would commit. He thought he would sacrifice to God his life and its pleasures, but God had disappointed him--since he had met with nothing but satisfaction in his new life.

He said we ought to establish ourselves within a sense of God's presence by continually conversing with Him. It would be shameful to quit His conversation, to think of unimportant and silly things.

We should feed and nourish our souls with sublime ideas about God; which would yield us great joy in being devoted to Him.

We ought to enliven our faith. It was sad we had so little faith, and that instead of taking faith for the standard of conduct, men amused themselves with unimportant matters which changed daily. The way of faith was the spirit of the church, and it was sufficient to bring us to a high degree of perfection.

We ought to give ourselves up to God, with regard both to worldly and spiritual things, and seek our satisfaction only in fulfilling His will, whether He lead us by suffering or by consolation, for all would be equal within a soul truly resigned to God. There needed to be faithfulness during those dry periods, insensitivities and irritabilities of times of prayer, by which God tries our love to Him. Those were the times for us to make good and effectual acts of resignation to His will, where one could promote spiritual advancement.

As for the miseries and sins he heard of daily in the world, he was so far from wondering at them, that, on the contrary, he was surprised there were not more, considering the malice that sinners were capable of. For his part, he prayed for sinners, but knowing that God could remedy the mischief they did when He desired, Brother Lawrence gave himself no further trouble about them.

To arrive at such resignation as God requires we should watch attentively over all our passions which intermingle: spiritual things as well as those of a carnal nature. God would give illumination concerning those passions to those who truly desire to serve Him.

Brother Lawrence thought: “If this was my design, sincerely to serve God, I might come to him as often as I pleased, without any fear of being troublesome; but if not, that I ought no more to visit him.”

Second Conversation

(Between Brother Lawrence and the Abbe de Beaufort)

1. Love is the Key Motive
2. Lawrence Experienced Fear and Anxiety
3. Then, Freedom and Joy

4. Confess to God
5. Live Simply with God
6. Trust in God

7. All Times are Times of Prayer
8. Self-Mortification is not Necessary
9. Take All Concerns to God

Brother Lawrence had always tried to be governed by love, without selfishness. Having resolved to make the love of God the end of all his actions, he had found reasons to be well satisfied with his way of doing things. He was glad when he could do something as simple as take up a piece of straw from the ground for the love of God, seeking Him only and nothing else, not even God's gifts.

He had long been troubled from a certain conviction that he was damned. All the men in the world could not have persuaded him to the contrary; but he had reasoned with himself about it: ie. "I did not engage in a religious life but for the love of God, and I have endeavored to act only for Him. Whatever becomes of me, whether I be lost or saved, I will always continue to act purely for the love of God. I shall have this good at least, that till death I shall have done all that is in me to love Him." That anxiety and trouble of mind had lasted four years; during which time he had suffered much.

Since that time he had passed his life in perfect freedom and continual joy. He confessed his sins between himself and God, as it were, to tell God that he did not deserve God's favors. Nevertheless, God still continued to bestow his favors in abundance.

Brother Lawrence said that in order to form the habit of conversing with God continually, and referring all we do to Him, we must first seek Him with some diligence. After taking care and doing this for some time, we would find His love inwardly exciting and bringing us to His presence without any difficulty.

Brother Lawrence expected that after the pleasant days God had given him he would have his turn with pain and suffering. But he was not anxious or uneasy about it, knowing very well that since he could do nothing by himself, God would not fail to give him the strength to bear them.

When the need arose to be virtuous, he addressed himself to God, saying, "Lord, I cannot do this unless You enable me." He then received more than sufficient strength.

When he had failed in certain duties, he confessed his fault to God, "I shall never do otherwise, if You leave me to myself. You must stop me from falling, and mend what is wrong." After this, he gave himself no further anxiety about it.

We ought to act with God in great simplicity, speaking to Him frankly and plainly, and imploring His assistance in all our affairs, even as they happen. God never failed to provide assistance, as Brother Lawrence had often experienced.

Brother Lawrence had been lately sent into Burgundy, to buy the supplies of wine for the monastery. He did not appreciate this task, since he did not like conducting business transactions, and because he had difficulty walking. He could not get around the boat except by rolling himself over the casks. However, he did not worry about the matter, nor about the purchase of the wine. He told God that it was God's business he was about and trusted in Him. Afterwards, he found that all had gone well. He had been sent into Auvergne the year before for the same reason, and that had also worked out well.

Likewise, in relation to Brother Lawrence's duties in the kitchen (to which he naturally had a great aversion), he made himself do everything there for the love of God, with prayer, upon all occasions. He asked for God's grace in order to do his work well. He then found that everything went more easily. That occurred during the fifteen years that he had been employed in the kitchen.

Brother Lawrence was well pleased with the job he now had at the monastery. However, he could go on with it or stop just as he could with the prior job, since in all matters he was obtaining satisfaction by doing small things for the love of God.

With Lawrence, dedicated times for prayer were not different from other times. He retired to pray according to the directions of his superior, but he did not necessarily want such times reserved nor ask for it. That was because his other activities and duties did not distract him from his focus upon God.

Brother Lawrence knew his obligation was to love God in all things, and he endeavored to do so. He indicated he had no need of a director to advise him, but he did need a confessor to absolve him. He was very sensible of his faults, but not discouraged by them. He confessed them to God, and did not plead with God to excuse them. Once he had confessed, he peaceably resumed his usual practice of love and adoration of God.

When Brother Lawrence was troubled in his mind, he consulted nobody, but knowing by the light of faith that God was present, he contented himself with directing all his actions toward God (i.e. doing them with a desire to please God, let what come what may).

Brother Lawrence understood that useless thoughts spoil everything. The mischief began there, but we ought to reject such thoughts as soon as we perceived their inappropriateness to what we were doing, and return to our communion with God.

Early in his time at the monastery he had often passed his time appointed for prayer in rejecting wandering thoughts, and then falling back into them. He could never regulate his devotion by certain techniques and methods as some do. At first he had meditated for some time, but afterwards the wandering thoughts stopped on their own, in a manner he could give no account of.

He had found that all bodily mortifications and other exercises were useless except if they serve to gain union with God by love. He had well understood this, and found that the shortest way to go straight to God was by a continual exercise of love, and by doing all things for God's sake.

He thought we ought to distinguish between the acts of understanding and those of the will. He believed that man's understanding was of comparatively little value, and that acts of faith and will were very valuable. He thought our primary purpose was to love and delight ourselves in God.

He thought all the possible kinds of mortification and penitence could not erase a single sin if they were without the love of God. We ought, without anxiety, to expect the forgiveness of our sins from the blood of Jesus Christ, endeavoring only to love Him with all our hearts. He thought God may have granted the greatest favors to the greatest sinners, as more noteworthy monuments of His mercy.

The greatest pains or pleasures of the world were not to be compared with what he had experienced of pain or pleasure in a spiritual state. So he was anxious for nothing and feared nothing. He desired but one thing of God--that he might not offend Him.

He had no anxieties and concerns--for he said, “When I fail in my duty, I readily acknowledge it, saying, I am used to doing so. I shall never do otherwise if I am left to myself. If I do not fail, then I give God thanks, acknowledging that it comes from Him.”

Third Conversation

(Between Brother Lawrence and the Abbe de Beaufort)

1. Faith Works Through Love
2. Practice God's Presence During All Activities

3. Resignation and Submission to God's Will
4. Love of God is Shown in Works and Virtue

Brother Lawrence stated that the foundation of spiritual life in him had been through a development of fear and awe of God through faith. Once he accomplished that he had no other concern but to faithfully focus every other thought so that he might perform all his actions for the love of God. When sometimes he had not thought of God for a good while, he did not reproach himself. After acknowledging his wretchedness to God, he returned to Him with greater trust because of his wretchedness for having forgotten Him.

He believed the trust we put in God honors Him a great deal, and brings great grace down upon us. It was impossible that God would deceive or let a soul suffer for long that is perfectly resigned to Him, and is resolved to endure everything for His sake.

Brother Lawrence had experienced the ready consolation of divine grace upon all occasions. Because of that experience and the resulting faith and confidence, when he had anything else to do, he did not become anxious regarding it beforehand. When it was time to do something, he found in God, as in a clear mirror, all that was appropriate for him to do. In recent years he had acted in this manner without worry or care, but by relying on God.

When other activities and concerns diverted him a little from the thought of God, a fresh reminder or thought came from God and indwelt his soul, and so inflamed and transported him that it was difficult for him to contain himself.

He found that he was often more united to God when practicing God's presence within his other activities and duties than when he practiced God's presence during the time set apart for meditation and prayer.

Brother Lawrence expected that he would experience great pain of body or mind in the future. However, he felt the worst that could happen to him was to lose the sense of God's presence which he had enjoyed so long. Nevertheless, he believed the goodness of God ensured that God would not forsake him, and that God would give him strength to bear whatever evil He permitted to occur to Brother Lawrence.

Consequently, he feared nothing, and had no occasion to consult with anybody about his state of being. When Lawrence had attempted to consult with others, he had always come away more confused. As he was ready to lay down his life for the love of God, he had no fear or sense of danger. He believed perfect resignation and submission to God's will was a sure way to heaven, a way in which we always have sufficient understanding and guidance for our conduct.

From the beginning of our spiritual lives we ought to be faithful in doing our duty and denying our selves. After that, unspeakable pleasures will follow. During difficult times we need only to have recourse to Jesus Christ, and to pray for His grace with which everything becomes easier.

Brother Lawrence thought that many do not advance in the Christian life because they focus on penances and spiritual exercises. However, they neglect the love of God which is the true goal. This neglect becomes clear within their works, and is the reason why we see so little solid virtue in people.

There is no need for either art or science to approach God, but only a heart resolutely determined to apply itself to nothing but God, for His sake, and to worship Him only.

Fourth Conversation

(Between Brother Lawrence and the Abbe de Beaufort)

1. How to Approach God
2. Wholehearted and Cheerful Renunciation
3. Praise, Adore and Love God

4. Pursue Holiness and Sanctification
5. Do All Things for the Love of God
6. The Importance of Faith, Hope and Charity

7. Suffering is Advantageous
8. Lawrence's Particular Experience
9. Pursuing God's Presence in His Job as Cook

Brother Lawrence spoke with me frequently and with openness of heart concerning his manner of approaching God. He told me that it consists in a wholehearted and cheerful renunciation of everything which does not lead to God. We need to accustom ourselves to a continual conversation with God, with freedom and in simplicity. We need only to recognize that God is intimately present with us, and to address ourselves to Him every moment.

We may pray for His assistance for knowing His will in doubtful things, and for rightly performing those things which we plainly see He requires of us. We can offer all that we do to Him before we do them, and give Him thanks after we have done them. In our conversation with God, we should praise, adore and love him incessantly, for His infinite goodness and perfection.

Without being discouraged on account of our sins, we should pray for His grace with a perfect confidence. We may rely upon the infinite merits of our Lord. God never fails to offer us His grace. Brother Lawrence regularly and distinctly perceived God's grace unless his thoughts had wandered from a sense of God's Presence or he had forgotten to ask God's assistance. God always gives us light when we are in doubt and when we have no other design but to please Him.

Our sanctification and holiness do not depend upon changing what we do, but in doing for God's sake what we commonly do for our own. It was sad to see how many people had mistaken the means for the end, addicting themselves to certain works which they performed very imperfectly because of their human or selfish regard. The most excellent method Lawrence had found of going to God was of doing all duties and activities without any view of pleasing men [Gal. 1:10; Eph. 6:5, 6.], and as far as possible purely for the love of God.

It was a great delusion to think that dedicated times of prayer ought to differ from other times. We are as strictly obliged to stay close to God during times of activity as during times of prayer. Brother Lawrence's prayer was nothing else than a continual sense of the presence of God, his soul being at that time insensible to everything but divine love. When appointed times of prayer were past he found no difference, because he still continued to be with God, praising and blessing Him with all his might. He thus passed his life in continual joy, yet hoped that God would give him suffering when he was stronger.

We should, once for all, heartily put our whole trust in God, and make a total surrender of ourselves to Him, secure that He will not deceive us. We should not be weary of doing small things for the love of God, who regards not the greatness of the work, but the love with which it is performed. We should not wonder if in the beginning we often fail in these endeavors, but that at last we should gain the habit which will naturally produce good consequences in us, without our care, and to our exceeding delight.

The whole substance of religion is faith, hope and charity. By their practice we become united to the will of God. All beside is indifferent and to be used as a means that we may arrive at our end, and be swallowed up by faith and charity. All things are possible to him who has faith. All is less difficult to him who hopes, and even more easy to him who loves. Persevere in the practice of these three virtues.

The goal we ought to propose to ourselves is to become in this life the most perfect worshippers of God we can possibly be--as we hope to be through all eternity. When we enter upon the spiritual we should consider and examine what we are. And then we should find ourselves worthy of all contempt, and not deserving the name of Christians. We are subject to all kinds of misery and innumerable events which trouble us, and cause constant fluctuations in our health and spirit and dispositions. We are persons whom God would humble with many pains and labors. We should not wonder that troubles and temptations, oppositions and contradictions happen to us. We ought, on the contrary, submit ourselves to those troubles and bear them as long as God pleases, as experiences which are highly advantageous to us.

The greater perfection to which a soul aspires, the more dependent it is upon divine grace. When he was questioned by a member of his monastery as to how he had attained such a habitual sense of God, Brother Lawrence told him that since his arrival at the monastery he had considered God as the focus of all his thoughts and desires, as the goal to which those thoughts and desires should approach and the end in which they should terminate.

At the beginning of his novitiate he spent the hours appointed for private prayer in thinking of God in order to convince his mind and impress upon his heart the nature of the divine existence. He did this through devotion and submission to the illumination of faith, rather than by reasoning and elaborate meditations. By this short and sure method, he practiced within himself the knowledge and love of God. He resolved to live in a continual sense of God's Presence, and if possible, never to forget Him.

Brother Lawrence filled his mind with prayers of great thoughts and feelings about the infinite being of God, and then went to his job in the kitchen since he was a cook for the monastery. There, after considering the various duties his job required and when and how each thing was to be done, he spent all the intervals of his time, as well as before and after his work in prayer.

When he began his job, he said to God with a childlike trust in Him, "O my God, since You are with me, and I must now, in obedience to Your commands, apply my mind to these other things, I pray You will grant me the grace to continue in Thy Presence. Please prosper me with Your assistance, receive all my work and possess all my affections." As he proceeded in his work, he continued his familiar conversation with his Creator, imploring His grace, and offering to Him all his actions.

When he had finished his work, he tried to determine how he had done. If he had done well, he thanked God. If otherwise, he asked pardon, and without being discouraged set his mind right again, and continued his exercise of the presence of God as if he had never strayed from it. "Thus," said he, "by rising after my falls, and by frequently renewed acts of faith and love, I have come to a state where it would be as difficult for me to not think of God as it was difficult for me to first become used to doing so."

As Brother Lawrence had found a profound benefit to walking in the presence of God, it was natural for him to recommend it earnestly to others. His example was a stronger inducement than any arguments he could propose. His very countenance was edifying. He had a sweet and calm devotion, as could not but affect those who saw and heard him. And it was observed that in the greatest hurry of work in the kitchen, he still preserved his mindset and heavenly focus. He was never hasty nor did he loiter, but did each thing in its appropriate time, with an even, uninterrupted composure and tranquility of spirit. "The time of activity," said he, "does not differ for me from the time of prayer. In the noise and clutter of my kitchen, while several persons are at the same time calling for different things, I possess God in as great tranquility as if I were upon my knees at the Blessed Sacrament."

First Letter

(Written by Brother Lawrence)

1. Cultivate God's Presence Habitually
2. Benefits of Cultivating His Presence

Since you desire so earnestly that I should communicate to you the method by which I arrived at the habitual sense of God's Presence which our Lord in His mercy has been pleased to grant to me. I must tell you that it is with great difficulty that I am prevailed on by your entreaties. I do it only upon the condition that you show my letter to no one else. If I knew that you would let it be seen, all the desire that I have for your spiritual uplift would not be able to make me send it to you. What I can tell you is that I found in many books different methods of approaching God, and different practices of the spiritual life. They served to confuse me rather than facilitate what I sought--which was how to become wholly God's.

This made me resolve to give my all for God. After giving myself wholly to God, in order to make all the satisfaction I could for my sins, I renounced, for love of Him, everything that was not Him. I began to live as if there was nothing and no one but God and me in the world. Sometimes I considered myself before Him as a poor criminal at the feet of his judge. At other times I considered Him in my heart as my Father, and as my God. I worshipped Him as often as I could, keeping my mind on His holy presence, and recalling it as often as I found it wandering from Him.

I found no small pain in this exercise, and yet I continued it, notwithstanding all the difficulties which occurred. I did not trouble or worry myself when my mind wandered involuntarily. I focused on His presence all the day long as well as at the appointed times of prayer; at all times, every hour, every minute, even at the busiest times of my work. I drove away from my mind everything that was capable of interrupting my thought of God.

Such has been my common practice ever since I entered into faith. Though I have done it very imperfectly, I have found great advantage through it. These, I well know, are to be imputed to the mercy and goodness of God, because we can do nothing without Him; and I less than any. But when we are faithful to keep ourselves in His holy presence, and set Him always before us, this not only stops our offending Him and doing anything that may displease Him, at least willfully, but it also provides us a holy freedom, and if I may so speak, a familiarity with God. By often repeating these acts, they become habitual, and the presence of God becomes natural to us.

Give Him thanks, if you please, with me, for His great goodness towards me, which I can never sufficiently admire, for the many favors He has done to so miserable a sinner as I am. May all things praise Him. Amen.

Second Letter

(Written by Brother Lawrence)

1. Practice God's Presence
2. Give Self up to God
3. God is Always With You
4. The Importance of Faith
5. First 10 Years Were Difficult
6. Walk Before God Simply, with Humility and Love

I have not found my practice of the presence of God and manner of life described in books that I have read. Although I have no great anxiety about my practice, for greater confidence I shall be glad to know your thoughts concerning it.

I had a conversation some days ago with a person of piety. He told me the spiritual life was a life of grace which begins with servile fear, which is increased by hope of eternal life, and is consummated by

pure love. He indicated each of these perspectives had its different stages by which one arrives at last at a blessed consummation.

I have not followed these types of perspectives and methods. On the contrary, from I know not what intuition, I found they discouraged me. This was the reason why, at my entrance into faith, I made a resolution to give myself up to God as the best satisfaction I could make for my sins. I decided to renounce all else besides for love of Him.

For the first years I commonly employed myself during the time set apart for devotion with thoughts of death, judgment, hell, heaven and my sins. I continued for a number of years applying my mind carefully during the rest of the day and even in the midst of my job, upon the presence of God, whom I considered as always with me, and as often within me.

Later, I came without realizing what I was doing to practice the same habits during my set time of prayer. This caused me great delight and consolation. This practice produced in me so high an esteem for God that faith alone was capable of satisfying me at that point. [Notation from the original: I suppose Brother Lawrence means that all distinct notions he could form of God were unsatisfactory, because he perceived them to be unworthy of God, and therefore his mind was not to be satisfied except by a view through faith, which apprehends God as infinite and incomprehensible, as He is in Himself, and not as He can be conceived by human ideas.]

Such was my beginning; and yet I must tell you that for the first ten years I suffered a great deal. I had the perception and worry that I was not devoted to God as I wished to be, and my past sins were always present in my mind. The great unmerited favors which God had provided me were the matter and source of my suffering. During this time I fell often and rose again. It seemed to me that creatures, reason and God Himself were against me. Faith alone was for me. I was troubled sometimes with thoughts that I had received favors because of my presumption—that I had presumed to arrive immediately where others arrive with difficulty. At other times I felt subject to a willful delusion, that there was no salvation for me.

When I thought about stopping my anxieties about these matters, I found myself changed all at once and suddenly. My worries did not diminish the trust I had in God, and they served only to increase my faith. My soul, which until that time was anxious, felt a profound inward peace, as if she were in her center and place of rest.

Ever since that time I walk before God simply, in faith, with humility and with love. I apply myself diligently to do nothing and think nothing which may displease Him. I hope that when I have done what I can, He will do with me what He pleases.

As for what occurs in my soul and mind at present, I cannot express it well. I have no pain or difficulty about my state, because I have no will but that of God. I endeavor to accomplish His will in all things, and to be resigned to His will. I would not take up a straw from the ground against His order, or from any other motive but purely that of love for Him.

I have stopped all methods of formal devotion and set prayers but those to which my practice causes me. I make it my business only to persevere in His holy presence, where I keep myself by a simple focus and a general fond regard for

God, which I believe is an actual presence of God. To describe it better, it is a habitual, silent, and secret conversation of the soul with God. It often causes joy and rapture inwardly and sometimes also outwardly. So great a joy and rapture that I am forced to control them, and prevent their appearance to others.

In short, I am assured beyond all doubt that my soul has been with God for more than thirty years. I pass over many things so I may not be tedious to you. Yet, I think it proper to inform you about how I think of myself before God, whom I behold as my King.

I consider myself as the most wretched of men, full of sores and corruption, someone who has committed all sorts of crimes against his King. Touched with appropriate regret, I confess to Him all my wickedness. I ask His forgiveness. I abandon myself in His hands so that He may do what He pleases with me. This King, full of mercy and goodness, very far from chastising me, embraces me with love, makes me eat at His table, serves me with His own hands and gives me the key to His treasures. He converses and delights Himself with me incessantly, in a thousand and a thousand ways, and treats me in all respects as His favorite.

This is how I consider myself in His holy presence. My most usual method is a simple attention and a general passionate regard for God. I often find myself attached to Him with greater sweetness and delight than that of an infant at the mother's breast. If I may dare to use the expression, I should choose to call this state the bosom of God, for the inexpressible sweetness which I taste and experience there. If sometimes my thoughts wander from it by necessity or infirmity, I am presently recalled by inward spiritual movements and feelings, so charming and delicious that I am ashamed to mention them.

I desire your reverence to reflect upon my great wretchedness, of which you are fully informed, than upon the great favors which God does me, all unworthy and ungrateful as I am.

As for my set hours of prayer, they are only a continuation of the same practice. Sometimes I consider myself as a stone before a carver, where he is to make a statue. I present myself thus before God, and desire Him to make His perfect image in my soul, and render me entirely like Himself.

At other times, when I apply myself to prayer, I feel all my spirit and all my soul lift up without any care or effort of mine. It continues as it were suspended and firmly fixed in God as its center and place of rest.

I know that some believe this state to be inactivity, delusion and self-love. I confess that it is a holy inactivity, and would be a happy self-love, if the soul in that state were capable of it. Because while the soul is in this repose, she cannot be disturbed by such acts as she was formerly accustomed, and which were then her support, but would now hinder her.

Yet I cannot bear that this should be called delusion; because the soul which thus enjoys God desires nothing but Him. If this be delusion, it belongs to God to remedy it. Let Him do what He pleases with me. I desire only Him, and to be wholly devoted to Him. You will, however, oblige me in sending me your opinion, to which I always pay a great deference, for I have a singular esteem for your reverence, and am yours in our Lord.

Third Letter

(Written by Brother Lawrence to Provide Advice and Support to a Soldier)

1. God is Gracious and Knows our Needs and Wants
2. Trust in God During Times of Danger
3. Short Remembrances are Acceptable to God

We have a God who is infinitely gracious and knows all our wants. I always thought that God might reduce you to extremity. He will come in His own time, and when you least expect it. Hope in Him more than ever. Thank Him with me for the favors He does you, particularly for the fortitude and patience which He gives you in your suffering. It is a plain mark of the care He takes of you. Comfort yourself then with Him, and give thanks for all.

I admire also the fortitude and bravery of [another individual who is a soldier]. God has given him a good disposition and a good will, but there is in him still a little of thc world and a great deal of youth. I hope the hardship which God has sent him will prove a wholesome remedy to him and make him enter into himself. It is an affliction very proper to cause him to put all his trust in God, who accompanies him everywhere.

Let him think of God as often as he can, especially during the greatest moments of battle and danger. A little lifting up the heart suffices. Little remembrances of God, acts of inward worship, and prayers however short, even while upon a march with a sword in hand, are nevertheless very acceptable to God. Far from lessening a soldier's courage during occasions of danger, they serve to fortify it.

Let him then think of God as much as he can. Let him accustom himself, by degrees, to this small but holy practice. Nobody else sees or senses it, and nothing is easier than to repeat often in the day these little internal adorations. Recommend to him, if you please, that he think of God as much as he can in the manner here directed. It is very fit and most necessary for a soldier who is daily exposed to the dangers of life, and often of salvation.

I hope that God will assist him and all the family, to whom I present my service, being theirs and yours.

Fourth Letter

(Letter Written by Brother Lawrence in the 3rd Person)

1. Practice the Presence of God
2. God Has Infinite Treasures to Share
3. There is No Time for Delay
4. Become Inflamed with Fervor

I have taken this opportunity to communicate to you the sentiments of one of our society concerning the admirable effects and continual assistances which he receives from the presence of God. Let you and me both profit by them.

For the more than forty years that he has spent in the faith, you must know this individual's continual pursuit has been to always be with God. He has not wanted to do anything, say anything or think anything which may displease God. All of this he has desired to do purely for the love of God, and because God deserves infinitely more.

This individual is now so accustomed to that divine presence that he receives from it continual benefit upon all occasions. For about thirty years his soul has been filled with joys so continual and sometimes so great that he is forced to use means to moderate them and to hinder their appearing outwardly. If at times he is a little absent from the divine presence, God makes Himself felt in his soul to recall him. This often happens when he is most engaged in his job and activities.

He answers with faithfulness to these inward callings, either by an elevation of his heart towards God, or by a meek and fond regard for Him. He uses those words which love forms upon these occasions. For instance, "My God, here I am devoted to Thee. Lord, make me according to Thy heart." Then it seems to him that this God of love, who is satisfied with such few words, reposes and rests in the depth and center of his soul. The experience of these things gives him a great assurance that God is always in the depth of his soul, and renders him incapable of doubting upon any account whatsoever.

Judge by this what contentment and satisfaction he may enjoy. He continually finds within himself this great treasure. He no longer anxiously searches after it, but has it open before him and may take what he pleases, when he pleases.

This individual complains much of our blindness, and cries often that we are to be pitied who content ourselves with much less. God, said he, has infinite treasure to bestow, and we occupy ourselves merely with small quantities of devotion which pass in a moment. Blind as we are, we hinder God and stop the flow of His grace. But when God finds a soul penetrated with a lively faith, He pours into it grace and favor plentifully. There they flow like a torrent. After being forcibly stopped from their ordinary course, grace and favor spread with impetuosity and abundance wherever they find openings and passageways.

Yes, we often stop this torrent, by the little value we set upon it. But let us stop it no more. Let us enter into ourselves and break down the barriers which hinder it. Let us make way for grace. Let us redeem the lost time, for perhaps we have but little time left. Death follows us closely, let us be well prepared for it. We die but once, and a miscarriage there is irretrievable.

I say again, let us enter into ourselves. The time presses. There is no room for delay. Our souls are at stake. I believe you have taken necessary measures, and that you will not be surprised. I commend you for it. It is the one thing necessary. We must, nevertheless, always work at it, because not to advance in the spiritual life is to go backward. But those who have the gale of the Holy Spirit within them go forward even in sleep. If the vessel of our soul is tossed with winds and storms, let us awake the Lord who reposes in it, and He will quickly calm the sea.

I have taken the liberty to impart to you these good sentiments, that you may compare them with your own. They will serve to kindle and inflame them if by misfortune (God forbid, for it would be a great misfortune) they should be cooled. Let us then both recall our first fervor. Let us profit by the example and the sentiment of this brother who is little known to the world, but known to God, and extremely caressed by Him. I will pray for you. Will you pray instantly for me, who am yours in our Lord.

Fifth Letter

(Written by Brother Lawrence)

1. Pray for a Sister Who is About to make a Profession of Faith
2. Carry on a Continual Conversation with God

I received two books and a letter from a Sister who is preparing to make her profession of faith. For that reason she desires the prayers of your holy society and your prayers in particular. I sense that she relies upon them a great deal. Please do not disappoint her. Pray to God that she makes her sacrifice in view of His love alone, and with a firm resolution to be wholly devoted to Him.

I will send you one of those books which speak of the presence of God, a subject which, in my opinion, contains the whole spiritual life. It seems to me that whoever practices it will soon become spiritually mature.

I know that for the right practice of the presence of God, the heart must be empty of all other things. This is so God will possess the heart alone. As He cannot possess it alone without emptying it of all besides, so neither can He act there and do in it what He pleases unless it be left open for Him.

There is not in the world a kind of life more sweet and delightful than that of a continual conversation with God. Only those who practice and experience it can comprehend it. Yet I do not advise you to do it from that motive. It is not pleasure which we ought to seek in this exercise. But let us do it from a principle of love, and because God would have us do so in this manner.

Were I a preacher, I should above all other things preach the practice of the presence of God; and were I a director, I should advise all the world to do it: so necessary do I think it, and so easy too.

Ah! If we but knew the need we have for the grace and assistance of God, we should never lose sight of Him. No, not for a moment. Make immediately a holy and firm resolution to never wilfully forget Him. Spend the rest of your days in His sacred presence, deprived for the love of Him if He thinks fit, of all consolations. Set heartily about this work, and if you do it as you ought, be assured that you will soon find out its consequences.

I will assist you with my prayers, poor as they are. I recommend myself earnestly to your prayers and those of your holy society.

Sixth Letter

(Written by Brother Lawrence)

1. Practice the Presence of God and Obtain Pleasure
2. Practice the Presence of God and Obtain Freedom

I have received from Mrs. [Unstated Name] the things you gave her to give to me. I wonder that you have not let me know your thoughts about the little book I sent to you, and which you must have received. I encourage you to full heartedly practice it in your old age. It is better late than never.

I cannot imagine how religious persons can live and be satisfied without the practice of the presence of God. For my part I keep myself with Him in the center of my soul as much as I can. When I am with Him I fear nothing, but the least turning away from Him is unbearable.

The practice of the presence of God does not fatigue the body. It is, however, proper to deprive the body sometimes, indeed often, of many little pleasures which are innocent and lawful. God will not permit that a soul which desires to be devoted entirely to Him should take other pleasures than with Him; that is more than reasonable.

I do not say that therefore we must put any violent constraint upon ourselves. No, we must serve God in a holy freedom. We must do our work and activities faithfully, without trouble or anxiety. We must recall our mind to God mildly and with tranquility, as often as we find it wandering from Him.

It is, however, necessary to put our whole trust in God, laying aside all other cares, and even some particular forms of devotion. These may be good in themselves, but one may engage in them unreasonably since those devotions are only means to attain an end. When by the exercise of the presence of God we are with Him who is our end, it may not be as useful to return to other means. We may continue with Him within a relationship of love, and persevere in His holy presence. We may do so by acts of praise and adoration and desire. We can do so by an act of resignation to His will and thanksgiving. We can practice His presence in all the different ways our spirit can invent.

Do not be discouraged by the aversion which you may feel arising from your human nature. You must do yourself a certain violence. At first, one may think practicing God's presence may be time which is lost. But you must go on and resolve to persevere in it until death, despite all the difficulties which may occur.

I recommend myself to the prayers of your holy society, and yours in particular. I am yours in our Lord.

Seventh Letter

(Written by Brother Lawrence)

1. Live and Die with God
2. Worship God with Confidence, Love and Humility

I pity and sympathize with you much. It will be of great importance if you can spend the remainder of your life worshiping God, and leave the care of your affairs to Him. He requires no great things of us: a little remembrance of Him from time to time, a little adoration, sometimes to pray for His grace, sometimes to offer Him your sufferings, and sometimes to give Him thanks for the favors He has given you.

He gives you favors in the midst of your troubles. Console yourself with Him as often as you can. Lift up your heart to Him even at your meals and when you are with others. The least little remembrance will always be acceptable to Him. You need not cry very loud, for He is nearer to us than we are aware.

It is not necessary to always be at church to be with God. We may make a silent speech with our heart, where we can retire from time to time to converse with Him in meekness, humility and love. Everyone is capable of such intimate conversation with God, some more, some less. He knows what we can do.

Let us begin then. Perhaps He expects but one generous and charitable resolution from us. Have courage. We have but little time to live. You are nearly 64, and I am almost 80. Let us live and die with God. Suffering will be sweet and pleasant to us while we are with Him, and the greatest pleasures will be a cruel punishment to us without Him. May He be praised and blessed. Amen.

Worship Him, beg His grace, offer Him your heart from time to time in the midst of all your work--every moment if you can. Do not always follow certain rules or set forms of devotion, but act with a general confidence in God, with love and humility.

You may be assured of my poor prayers, and that I am their servant, and yours particularly.

Eighth Letter

(Written by Brother Lawrence)

1. Confess Your Sins and Faults, and Humble Yourself
2. How to Address Wandering Thoughts

You are telling me nothing new. You are not the only one who is troubled with wandering thoughts. Our mind naturally roves about. As the will is mistress of all our faculties, she must recall such wandering thoughts and carry them to God as their last end.

The mind is not sufficiently focused when we first engage in devotion and worship. The mind develops certain bad habits of wandering and dissipation which are difficult to overcome, and commonly draw us even against our wills to the things of the earth.

I believe one remedy for this is to confess our sins and faults, and humble ourselves before God. I do not advise you to use many words in prayer. Many words and long discourses are often the times when wandering thoughts occur. Use few words and be willing to be silent and still in prayer and devotion before God, like a mute or paralytic beggar at a rich man's gate.

Let it be your business to keep your mind within the presence of the Lord. If your mind sometimes wanders and withdraws itself from Him, do not become anxious. Trouble, anxiety and rumination tend to distract the mind, rather than allowing one to gather oneself and refocus. Our wills must bring our minds back into tranquility. If you persevere in this manner, God will have pity on you.

One way to refocus the mind easily in the time of prayer and preserve it in tranquility is to prevent it from wandering too far at other times. Keep your mind strictly in the presence of God, and be accustomed to think of Him often. You will then find it easy to keep your mind calm in the time of prayer, or at least to refocus it from its wanderings.

I have told you already in detail within my former letters of the advantages we may draw from this practice of the presence of God. Let us pursue this practice seriously and pray for one another.

Ninth Letter

(Written by Brother Lawrence)

1. Letter to a Sister
2. Think of God

I have enclosed a letter which is an answer to the letter which I received from [a Sister in a religious order]. Please deliver it to her. She seems to me full of good will, but she would like to go faster than grace. One does not become holy all at once. I recommend her to you. We ought to help one another by our advice, and yet more by our good examples. You will assist me, if you tell me of her from time to time, and whether she is fervent and obedient.

Sister,

Let us think often that our only business in this life is to please God. All besides may well be folly and vanity. You and I have lived more than forty years in faith and within a monastic life. Have we employed them in loving and serving God--who by His mercy has called us to this state and for that particular end? I am filled with shame and confusion when I reflect on the great favors which God has done and continues to do for me. For I believe I have made a bad use of them, and have advanced only slightly in the way of perfection.

Since by His mercy God gives us a little more time, let us begin in earnest and make up for lost time. Let us return with full assurance to our Father of mercies who is always ready to receive us affectionately. Let us renounce--let us full heartedly renounce for the love of Him all that is not Him. God deserves infinitely more. Let us think of Him perpetually. Let us put all our trust in Him. I do not doubt but that we shall soon find the effect of it in receiving His abundant grace. Through his grace we can do all things and without it we can do nothing but sin.

We cannot escape the dangers which abound in life without the actual and continual help of God. Let us then pray to Him continually. How can we pray to Him without being with Him? How can we be with Him except by thinking of Him often? And how can we think of Him often, except by the holy habit which we should form?

You will tell me that I am always saying the same thing. It is true, for this is the best and easiest method I know. As I use no other, I advise all the world to do it. We must know before we can love. In order to know God, we must often think of Him. When we come to love Him, we shall then also think of Him often, for our heart will be with our treasure. This is an argument which well deserves your consideration.

Tenth Letter

(Written by Brother Lawrence)

1. Be Happy in Your Trust in God
2. Loss of a Friend may Lead to Closeness to God

I have had a good deal of difficulty in bringing myself to write to Mr. [Unstated Name]. I do it now purely because you and Madam desire me to do so. Pray write in the address and send it to him. I am very well pleased with the trust which you have in God. I wish that He may increase it in you more and more. We cannot have too much trust in so good and faithful a Friend. He will never fail us in this world nor in the next.

If Mr. [Unstated Name] takes advantage of the loss of a friend he has had and puts all his confidence in God, he will soon find that he has another friend who is more powerful and more inclined to serve him. God deals with people and their hearts and souls as He desires. Perhaps Mr. [Unstated Name] was too much attached to the friend he lost. We ought to love our friends, but without encroaching upon the love of God which must be our principal desire and focus.

Please remember what I have recommended to you--which is to think often about God. Do so by day and by night and in all that you do, including conversations with others and pleasures and entertainments. God is always near you and with you. Do not leave Him alone.

You would think it rude to leave a friend alone who had come to visit you. Why then would you neglect or leave God alone? Do not forget Him, but think about Him often. Adore Him continually. Live and die with Him. This is the glorious employment of a Christian. In a word, this is our profession. If we do not yet know it, we must learn it.

I will endeavor to support you with my prayers, and am yours in our Lord.

Eleventh Letter

(Written by Brother Lawrence)

1. Pray that God will Give You Strength to Bear Pain and Illness
2. God is the Physician of the Body and the Soul
3. Be at Peace Where God Places You

I do not pray that you may be delivered from your pain and suffering. I pray to God earnestly that He will give you strength and patience to bear them as long as He pleases. Comfort yourself with Him who holds you fastened to the cross. He will free you when He thinks fit. Happy are those who suffer with Him. Accustom yourself to suffer in that manner, and seek from Him the strength to endure as much and as long as He shall judge it to be necessary for you.

The men of the world do not comprehend these truths, and that is not to be wondered at. They suffer as men of nature and not like followers of Christ. They consider sickness as a pain and burden for their nature and not as a favor from God. Seeing it only in that light, they find nothing in it but grief and distress. However, those who consider sickness as coming from the hand of God, as the effect of His mercy and the means which He employs for their salvation, commonly find in it great sweetness and sensible consolation.

I wish you could convince yourself that God is often nearer to us and more effectually present with us in sickness than in health. Rely upon no other Physician. According to my impression and conviction, He reserves your cure to Himself.

Put all your trust in Him, and you will soon find the effect of it in your recovery. We often slow down recovery by putting greater confidence in medicine than in God.

Whatever remedies you make use of, they will succeed only so far as He permits. When pains come from God, He only can cure them. He often sends diseases of the body to cure those of the soul. Comfort yourself with the sovereign Physician of the soul and body.

I foresee that you will tell me that it is easy for me to say these things since I am not suffering, and that I am eating and drinking at the table of the Lord. You have reason to say so. However, would it not be painful to the greatest criminal in the world to eat at the King's table, and be served by Him, and despite such favor be without assurance of pardon? I believe such a criminal would feel exceeding great anxiety, which nothing could moderate except trust in the goodness of his sovereign. So I assure you, that whatever pleasures I taste at the table of my King, yet my sins, ever present before my eyes, as well as the uncertainty of my pardon, torment me, though in truth that torment itself is pleasing.

Be satisfied and at peace with the condition in which God places you. However happy you may think me, I envy you. Pains and suffering would be a paradise to me if I should suffer with my God. The greatest pleasure would be hell to me if I should experience them without Him. All my consolation is to suffer something for His sake.

I must in a little time go to be with God. What comforts me in this life is that I now see Him by faith. I see Him in such a manner as might make me say I believe no more, but I see. I feel what faith teaches us, and in that assurance and practice of faith, I will live and die with Him.

Continue then always with God. It is the only support and comfort for your affliction. I shall beseech Him to be with you. I present you with my service.

Twelfth Letter

(Written by Brother Lawrence)

1. Entertain Yourself with God and His Company
2. Faith is Our Support and Confidence
3. God Never Forsakes Us

If we were well accustomed to the exercise of the presence of God, all bodily diseases would be much alleviated. God often permits that we should suffer a little to purify our souls, and teaches us to continue in His presence and in faith.

Take courage. Offer Him your pains constantly. Pray to Him for strength to endure them. Above all, get into the habit of entertaining yourself often with God's company. Forget Him as little as possible. Adore Him in your infirmities. Offer yourself to Him over and over. In the height of your sufferings, beseech Him humbly and affectionately--as a child would his father--to make you conformable to His holy will. I shall endeavor to assist you with my poor prayers.

God has many ways of drawing us to Him. He sometimes hides Himself from us. Faith alone, which will not fail us in time of need, ought to be our support and the foundation of our confidence. Our confidence must be in God.

I do not know how God will dispose of me. I am always happy. All the world suffers, and I, who deserve the severest discipline, feel joys so continual and so great that I can scarce contain them.

I would willingly ask of God a part of your sufferings. I know my weakness, which is so great, that if He left me one moment to myself, I should be the most wretched man alive. And yet I know He will not leave me alone, because faith gives me as strong a conviction as any sense can, that He never forsakes us. Let us fear to leave Him. Let us always be with Him. Let us live and die in His presence.

Do pray for me, as I do for you.

Thirteenth Letter

(Written by Brother Lawrence)

1. Consolation for Suffering
2. Trust in God for Strength
3. God Treats the Body and the Soul

I am in pain to see you suffer so long. What gives me some consolation and sweetens the feeling I have of your grief, is that they are proofs of God's love towards you. See them in that way and you will bear them more easily. Given how things are, it is my opinion that you should…resign yourself entirely to the providence of God. Perhaps He waits only for that resignation and a perfect trust in Him to cure you. Despite all your cares, medicine has so far proved unsuccessful, and your malady still increases. It will not be tempting God to submit and abandon yourself in His hands, and expect all from Him.

I told you in my last letter that God sometimes permits bodily diseases to cure the maladies of the soul. Have courage then. Make a virtue of necessity. Ask of God, not deliverance from your pains, but strength to bear them resolutely for the love of Him--all that He should require, and as long as He shall require.

Such prayers, indeed, are a little hard for human nature, but most acceptable to God, and sweet to those that love Him. Love sweetens pain, and when one loves God, one suffers for His sake with joy and courage. I beseech you to comfort yourself with Him, who is the only Physician of all our maladies. He is the Father of the afflicted, always ready to help us. He loves us infinitely more than we can imagine. Love Him then, and seek not consolation anywhere else. I hope you will soon receive it. Goodbye. I will help you with my prayers, poor as they are. I shall be, always, yours in our Lord.

Fourteenth Letter

(Written by Brother Lawrence)

1. Give Thanks to God
2. Have Familiar, Humble and Affectionate Conversations with God
3. Persevere to Gain the Right Attitude

I give thanks to our Lord for having relieved you a little, according to your desire. I have often been near death, though I was never so much satisfied as at those times. Accordingly, I did not pray for relief, but I prayed for strength to suffer with courage, humility and love. Ah, how sweet is it to suffer with God! However great the sufferings may be, receive them with love. It is paradise to suffer and be with Him.

If we would enjoy the peace of paradise even within this life, we must accustom ourselves to a familiar, humble and affectionate conversation with Him. We must stop our spirit from wandering away from Him upon any occasion. We must make our heart a spiritual temple where we adore Him incessantly. We must watch continually over ourselves so that we will not do or say or think anything which will displease Him. When our minds are employed in that manner in relation to God, suffering will become as a balm and consolation.

I know that it is difficult to arrive at this state of mind and attitude. We must act purely in faith. But though it is difficult, we know also that we can do all things with the grace of God, which He never refuses to those who ask for it earnestly. Knock and persevere in knocking, and I tell you that God will open the door to you in His due time. He will grant you all at once what He has deferred during many years. Goodbye. Pray to God for me, as I pray to Him for you. I hope to see Him quickly.

Fifteenth Letter

(Written by Brother Lawrence From His Deathbed)

1. God Knows What Is Best For Us
2. Pursue Knowledge and Intimacy With God
3. Seek and Love God by Faith, and Not For His Blessings
4. Pray For One Another

God knows best what is necessary for us, and all that He does is for our good. If we knew how much He loves us, we should always be willing to receive equally and with indifference the sweet and the bitter from Him. Everything which comes from Him would please.

The greatest sufferings never seem intolerable, except when we see them in the wrong light. When we see our suffering as being dispensed by God, and when we know that it is our loving Father who abases and distresses us, our sufferings will lose their bitterness and even become a matter of consolation.

Let all our work and effort be to know God. The more one knows Him, the more one desires to know Him. Since knowledge and intimacy is commonly the measure of love, the deeper and more extensive our knowledge and intimacy the greater will be our love. If our love of God is great we will love Him equally in pain and pleasure.

Let us not seek or love God in order to obtain blessings or favors (however noble or spiritual). Such blessings and favors cannot bring us as near to God as faith does in one simple act. Let us seek Him often by faith. He is within us. Do not seek Him elsewhere. Are we not rude and deserving of blame if we leave God alone, in order to busy ourselves about unimportant matters which do not please Him and perhaps offend Him? It is to be anticipated that these unimportant matters will one day cost us much.

Let us begin to be devoted to Him in earnest. Let us cast everything else out of our hearts. He would possess our hearts alone. Beg that He would do so. If we do what we can, we shall soon see that transformation of our beings to which we aspire.

I cannot thank Him sufficiently for the peace He has provided you. I hope that through His mercy I will see Him within a few days. Let us pray for one another.

Brother Lawrence took to his bed two days later, and died within the week.

Afterword

Old Age

Most of us have to face and come to terms with old age and debility. All of us have to face and come to terms with death. People close to me in my family are becoming old and nearing death. My parents are semi-retired, but continue to be active in their Christian ministry. Many of the people my parents have known and ministered to are passing away. With their own health issues increasing, they have adjusted their daily and weekly schedules. They are slowing, but active and working in their seventies and eighties.

My father had his first inkling of mortality in his mid-fifties, presenting to his doctor with shortness of breath. An angiogram showed him to have multiple blockages in the arteries of his heart. He has gone on to have two angioplasties, and takes a cocktail of pharmaceuticals to keep his coronary artery disease in control. My mother has had a number of medical issues since her fifties. They have progressed over the years, debilitating her, caused pulmonary compromise, hospitalization for life threatening pneumonia, deterioration of joints and severe chronic pain. She has had cognitive and personality changes contributed to by her medical conditions and medications. Neither their times or beings are easy. As they have grown older, my parents pray many times a day, and have a Bible study for two hours every morning. As they slow, they are spending more time with God, making Him a larger part of their days and activities and thoughts. Their comfort and resilience are coming from the company they keep.

Dementia

One member of my family has Alzheimer's disease which is cutting away at his memories, his person and personality. He is becoming more passive and general. He is blind in his right eye and almost blind in his left. He runs into or trips over objects he did not see in his peripheral vision. He has fallen heavily, with the weight and decreased mobility he has gained with age. He has become incontinent, and uses adult diapers. I notice him sticking his face close to television screens to see programs he loves, good feeling shows about families like the *Waltons* or *Little House on the Prairie* which are a comfort to him.

I help him shave sometimes. He stares straight ahead into the mirror. I take his electric razor with my right hand, and hold his face, while curving my left arm around the back of his head. Afterward, I clean his face and throat, using a warm washcloth. Then, I place a dollop of lotion in my hand and rub it into his jaw and cheeks. How does that feel, I ask. Good, he says and smiles.

The Alzheimer's disease and blindness may be closing the world about him, making him more isolative and tentative. He is quieter. His brain is changing, and his comments and I suspect his thoughts are coursing along fewer, well known paths. Certain compulsive traits which were subtle before are becoming more pronounced: his daily entries of the day and month on a piece of paper, his regimented manner of completing his toiletries in the mornings. He does less, sleeps more, and remains in his room longer. He talks to himself and to God for long periods of time. What is his awareness of God? How does he feel God's overwhelming love and mercy. He seems to sense and be within God's presence more now than when he was young.

Death

I have been privileged to be present at the very end of a person's life. I visited a woman I did not know well who was dying of cancer, whose cognition was affected by her medications for pain. There were no other visitors there, and I do not know what had occurred in her life to bring her to an end where she was alone. Were family and friends gone, or were they distant? She began to speak, and I sat and listened for a short time into the night. There seemed to be little capacity for real dialogue. I do not know, but perhaps she was aware I was in the room with her, listening to what she might say or communicate. She was not clear, not easy to understand. She spoke of a husband, possibly of a child and of being younger, in fragments, perhaps with thoughts and memories intertwining. Her brain and being, unconscious and conscious, seemed to be expressing themselves, for one of the last times on this earth. I tried to respond in ways which were supportive, acknowledging and affirming. Finally, in a moment of quietness, I had a distinct sense of the presence of God, and I wondered if she had been aware of His presence throughout, and been listening and speaking to Him.

Sharing & Reviews

If this book has been helpful or a blessing, please share it with friends, and members of your family and community.

I would also greatly appreciate your review of this book at appropriate sites. Please use the title name *Practice of the Presence of God with Devotional & Study Guide*. Please use both relevant author names: Brother Lawrence and J. D. Nelson. Thank you for your time and consideration.

58806868R00046

Made in the USA
Columbia, SC
24 May 2019